Cambridge **Discovery Education**™

▶ **INTERACTIVE READERS**

Series editor: Bob Hastings

MONEY TREE
THE BUSINESS OF ORGANICS

B2+

Caroline Shackleton and Nathan Paul Turner

CAMBRIDGE
UNIVERSITY PRESS

Discovery
EDUCATION™

CAMBRIDGE UNIVERSITY PRESS
Cambridge, New York, Melbourne, Madrid, Cape Town,
Singapore, São Paulo, Delhi, Mexico City

Cambridge University Press
32 Avenue of the Americas, New York, NY 10013-2473, USA

www.cambridge.org
Information on this title: www.cambridge.org/9781107636781

First published 2014

Printed in Hong Kong, China, by Golden Cup Printing Company Limited

A catalog record for this publication is available from the British Library.

Library of Congress Cataloging-in-Publication Data

Shackleton, Caroline.
 Money tree : the business of organics / Caroline Shackleton and Nathan
Paul Turner.
   pages cm. -- (Cambridge discovery interactive readers)
  ISBN 978-1-107-63678-1 (pbk. : alk. paper)
 1. Organic farming--Juvenile literature. 2. English language--Textbooks for foreign speakers.
 3. Readers (Elementary) I. Title.

S605.5.S52 2013
631.5'84--dc23

                          2013021202

ISBN 978-1-107-63678-1

Additional resources for this publication at www.cambridge.org

Layout services, art direction, book design, and photo research: Q2ABillSMITH GROUP
Editorial services: Hyphen S.A.
Audio production: CityVox, New York
Video production: Q2ABillSMITH GROUP

Contents

Before You Read:
Get Ready!

Natural products are more popular than ever before, but how natural are they? We take a look at some of the many ways of going organic.

Words to Know

Complete the sentences with the correct words.

soil

pest

fertilizer

urban garden

whole foods

1 A place to grow food in a city or a town is an _____ .

2 Foods that are not changed in any way by adding something to them or taking something out of them are called _____ .

3 An insect or small animal that is harmful to crops is a _____ .

4 A natural or chemical product that is spread on land in order to make plants grow well is called _____ .

5 The material in which plants grow is _____ .

Words to Know

Read the paragraph. Then complete the definitions with the correct highlighted words.

In the second half of the 20th century, the debate about how we should look after the land around us became more and more serious as populations grew, and new industrial farming techniques, including the frequent use of pesticides, began to be used. The first organic pioneers questioned this new way of farming. They were early critics of techniques that most people thought were positive. Their criticisms came from a belief that to rob from the land without giving nutrients back was not ethical. Today, many organic farmers see themselves as activists in the fight for a healthier planet.

1 _____ : what plants or animals need in order to live and grow

2 _____ : a person who expresses disagreement with something or disapproval of someone

3 _____ : a serious discussion between two persons or groups with different opinions about something

4 _____ : a person who works to achieve political or social change, especially as a member of an organization

5 _____ : a person who is among the first to do, study, or develop something

6 _____ : relating to principles of right and wrong

7 _____ : chemicals used to kill pests

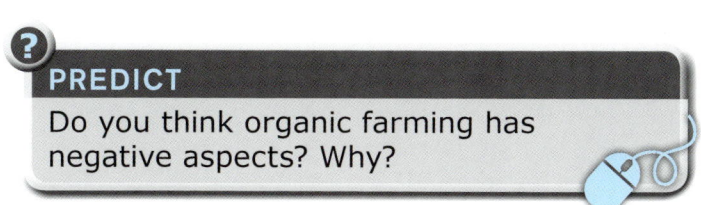

? PREDICT

Do you think organic farming has negative aspects? Why?

CHAPTER 1

Whole Foods

CAN A SUPERMARKET REALLY BE ORGANIC?

In 1980, John Mackey, a 27-year-old vegetarian, and his 23-year-old girlfriend, Renee Lawson, were running a small health food business in Austin, Texas, USA. They decided the time was right for an organic supermarket, so they merged[1] their business with another store and opened Whole Foods Market. Their motto[2] was: Whole Foods, Whole People, Whole Planet.

Previously, health food stores had concentrated on **herbal** products, beans, fruits, and vegetables; but the new store also sold products such as fresh bread and local fish, meat, and cheese. The new supermarket was an immediate success and by 1985, Whole Foods had added stores in Dallas and Houston.

[1]**merge:** combine two or more companies
[2]**motto:** a phrase that expresses the beliefs of an organization

The company began buying out its local competitors, and in 1992, it started opening stores throughout the USA. Since then, its varied organic produce, clean colorful stores, and friendly staff have proved a recipe for success.

The Whole Foods success story has not been free of criticism, however. Although the company sells an image of high quality organic, local produce, the reality is often different. Most organic food in the USA actually comes from a few giant farms. This is because US food legislation[3] makes it difficult for small farms to qualify[4] as "organic."

Also, a lot of the company's produce comes from abroad; and while goods from China and Mexico may be green, the amount of oil needed to transport them is certainly not. Many green activists insist that Whole Foods does not represent the model of **sustainable** local food that the organic pioneers intended.

One of the biggest criticisms of the store, however, is its pricing. In fact, the company's promotion of healthy organic food as a lifestyle choice to the wealthy has even led some critics to change its motto to: "Whole Foods, Whole Paycheck . . ."

[3]**legislation:** a law or set of laws
[4]**qualify:** If you qualify for something, you are allowed to do it.

CHAPTER 2

What Is Organic Anyway?

WHEN YOU THINK OF ORGANIC FOOD, WHAT WORDS COME TO MIND? NATURAL, LOCAL, ETHICAL? IN FACT, THE CLASSIFICATION OF ORGANIC FOOD IS A TRICKY BUSINESS.

Until the 19th century, nobody would have considered farming as anything other than organic. Crops were fertilized using animal manure and compost. In the 18th and 19th centuries, however, chemists were discovering more about chemicals. The work of German chemist Justus von Liebig, in particular, led to the development of cheap nitrogen[5] fertilizers. The agricultural revolution that followed, especially in Great Britain, brought about a huge increase in crop production. This helped feed the country's rapidly growing urban population and reduce famine.[6] However, not everybody was convinced of the benefits of the new technologies.

[5]**nitrogen:** a gas, one of the chemical elements
[6]**famine:** an extreme lack of food in a region, causing suffering and death

Sir Albert Howard's experiences in India convinced him that correct animal and crop management in a local area produced strong pest-resistant[7] plants that were superior to those grown with chemical fertilizers. He saw chemical fertilizers as expensive, unnecessary, and unsustainable and studied ways to farm productively but naturally.

Howard himself never used the word organic. It was British agriculturalist Lord Northbourne who first referred to a farm as a single "organic whole," describing a more balanced, sustainable style of farming. Northbourne's ideas, however, were not widely accepted. The following years saw an increase in the use of fertilizers and pesticides, which allowed farmers to plant large quantities of single crops. Most farms became industrialized single-crop producers that depended on pesticides and fertilizers. Then in the 1970s, some people began to express their concerns about the negative effects of these methods on soil quality and the environment. These green activists began to call for a return to more traditional styles of farming.

....

[7] **pest-resistant:** not easily damaged by pests

? EVALUATE

Was the use of pesticides and fertilizers more beneficial than harmful? Why?

At the same time, in other parts of the world modern methods were replacing traditional farming. In Mexico, Pakistan, and India, Nobel prize-winning agriculturalist Norman Borlaug pioneered the use of new crops and technologies and greatly increased food production. Environmentalists criticized Borlaug's work, which they claimed led to reliance on a single crop, inequality, malnutrition,[8] and the loss of natural wildlife. While Borlaug recognized some of these claims, he argued that his principle aim was an end to hunger, something, he pointed out, that most of his critics had never experienced.

Meanwhile in the USA and the UK, many smaller farms were trying to return to natural methods, growing many different crops and keeping animals to fertilize the soil. Throughout the 1970s, activists continued to promote a return to more traditional ways of living, and some people were encouraged to try to provide their own food, both out in the countryside and using smaller urban gardens.

[8] **malnutrition:** bad health caused by having too little food

However, as the idea of organic food became more popular, big business began to move in.

The 1980s and 1990s saw the growth of large organic farms and supermarkets, and the importation of organic produce from abroad. At the same time, new legislation in places such as the USA and Europe has made it extremely expensive and complicated for small producers to obtain organic certification. Ironically, many natural local farms are not classed as organic, while much of the organic food supermarkets sell often comes from foreign countries. This has led to criticism from environmentalists who feel that the term organic no longer represents the ideals of organic farming.

As we move into the 21st century with a world population of seven billion people, the debate on how we should feed ourselves shows no sign of coming to an end.

Video Quest

Organic Farming

Watch the video about local organic farming. What are the benefits of eating locally grown food?

CHAPTER 3

Agribusiness vs. Organic Farming

THE DEBATE ABOUT THE MEANING OF "NATURAL"

The pioneers of organic farming of the early and mid-twentieth century saw the movement as a return to small family-sized, local farms and a rejection[9] of the big business model of large farms. Organic farming was a way of protecting the local environment, but also of freeing human beings from the "rat race" of modern consumer society.

[9] **rejection:** not accepting or agreeing with something

In the USA, these ideas were often linked to the pioneer spirit[10] of the 19th century, which was seen as a golden age of simplicity and the good life. In the 1960s and 1970s, more and more people rejected life in the cities and moved back to the countryside to live on small farms with the dream of providing for themselves.

However, the last 25 years or so have seen a dramatic change in organic farming. California, sometimes known as the Green State, is a good example. In 1972, there were just two large farms producing organic food in California. But by the 1990s, many traditional farms started to change over to organic produce.

These new companies, however, were mainly interested in making a **profit**. Large commercial farms could out-produce the smaller family farms and sell their products more cheaply to supermarkets that were lining up to buy into the profitable organic market. There was a growing need for new legislation to control the organic produce being imported and sold in supermarkets. In 1990, the USA introduced new legislation on the production and sale of organic food.

[10] **spirit:** a state of mind or attitude

Many small farms found it impossible to apply for the new organic certification, even if they were farming organically, as the certificate required frequent, expensive inspections.[11] Many smaller and part-time businesses could not now legally sell their goods as "organic," but as "garden produce" or "fresh and local." In response, many small producers began to get together to help each other sell their produce without using the "organic" label. They formed local groups and organized small traditional markets, which became known as "Farmers' Markets."

Held monthly or weekly, these markets were usually advertised to the general public as a way of trying and buying fresh, local products. They were also a way producers could talk directly to consumers about organic food production. The producers could charge lower prices, providing an affordable way for their customers to eat healthy fresh produce.

....

[11] **inspection:** a careful examination by an official to make certain that something is in good condition, or that rules are being obeyed

Currently, there are more than 300 farmers' markets in New York alone, and they are gaining popularity in other parts of the world, such as the Netherlands, Germany, and the UK. A market tradition once in danger of being lost is returning to many cities. This has led to a number of movements promoting fresh local produce, such as the SlowFood movement that began in Europe, and the Locavore movement in the USA.

The Internet has helped to create a renaissance[12] in kitchen gardening. Sometimes called urban gardening, kitchen-gardening involves using backyards and gardens for food production. Many people have returned to keeping their own chickens.

[12] **renaissance:** a new growth or interest in something

Video Quest

The Locavore Movement

Watch this video about eating local food. How far do non-local products travel?

CHAPTER 4

Organopónicos

CUBA'S ECO-FRIENDLY REVOLUTION

For most of the twentieth century Cuba was famous for two things; cigars and rum. The first, supposedly the finest in the world, came from its large tobacco plantations. The second came from its most important crop, cane sugar.

After Cuba freed itself from Spain in 1898, it came under the political and economic influence of the USA. Large US companies encouraged local landowners to concentrate on producing sugar and to ignore food crops, which could be imported from the USA. This made Cuba depend economically on the USA for its basic needs.

After the Cuban Revolution of 1959, the USA placed a strict trade embargo[13] on Cuba, causing serious food shortages. So the Cuban government turned to the Soviet Union for help.

[13]**trade embargo:** a government order to temporarily stop trading certain goods or with certain countries

From this point on, Cuba produced sugar for the Soviet Union and imported much of its food and agricultural technology from there in return.

However, with the sudden fall of the Soviet Union in 1991, Cuba lost its main trading partner. The US trade embargo was still in place, and Cuba found itself without enough food to feed its people. The United Nations estimated that people's daily food intake fell by thirty to fifty percent. The situation was extremely serious, and the Cuban government needed to react fast.

The solution was to turn sugar plantations into fields for growing food. People were also encouraged to produce food locally by growing their own crops in small urban gardens. This food was necessarily organic, as nothing remained of the chemical fertilizers and pesticides previously imported from the Soviet Union. Without these chemical products, Cubans had to learn new methods, and re-learn some of the old ways, too.

The government provided teachers and courses to help people learn organic farming techniques. These included the use of earthworms to create soil nutrients, plant-oil pesticides, and predator[14] insects to kill pests. Crop **rotation** kept soil nutrients high and avoided over-farming.

[14]**predator:** an animal that hunts and kills other animals for food

These urban gardens quickly became known as *organopónicos*, in reference to their replacement of Soviet hydroponic technology. Soviet *hydroponics*, a method where plants are grown in containers of specially fertilized water, had been an important part of Cuban farming. Without chemical fertilizers, the hydroponic method was thought to be useless. But amazingly, the Cubans soon had the systems working again, replacing the chemical fertilizers with local organic nutrients, including cane sugar.

The new system was extremely effective. In just a few years, there were almost 200 urban gardens covering 35,000 hectares in the capital, Havana, alone.

They provided more than ninety percent of the city's food. Production went up from four kilograms per square meter to 24 kilograms, all without the use of chemicals. Some of these gardens were run by the state, but many others were started by people in their own gardens to help provide food. The state also provided some organic products such as organic pesticides, **seeds**, and irrigation[15] materials. There are now more than 7,000 *huertos* or gardens, throughout the country, and in Havana itself, only organic farming is allowed.

Although the Cuban "organoponic revolution" was based on necessity rather than choice, environmentalists have celebrated it as a huge step forward in showing what can be achieved with organic methods. Cuba's success shows that it's possible for a whole country to feed itself without help and even improve production, using small local gardens and no chemicals. This system is now being tried in other parts of Central and South America, such as Venezuela.

....
[15]**irrigation:** a system to supply land with water so that crops and plants will grow or grow better

CHAPTER 5

Going Organic – Is It Worth It?

WHAT'S THE REAL COST OF BEING ORGANIC?

"Organic": in less than a century, the term has become a symbol of quality and tradition. Nowadays, we are offered a wealth of organic products never imagined by organic pioneers. In recent years, products have appeared in shopping areas and superstores claiming to be "100% organic," or to contain "no artificial additives." From salads to skincare products, shoppers have an incredible range to choose from.

But how much better are those products than non-organic products? Do they really help protect the environment? Are they better for your health? The one thing you can be sure about is that they'll probably cost twice as much! So how can you know what you're getting and whether it's worth it?

The largest sector of organic products is still food, both as separate products and as ingredients in everything from breakfast cereals to ice-cream. Supporters claim that these products taste better and are better for you. Critics say there is no **nutritional** difference.

In recent years, public demand for these products has increased enormously, driven by scares over the possible health risks of chemical pesticides. However, the debate continues over whether or not these risks really exist. Both sides present evidence from scientific studies. First, consumers are told that pesticides can cause cancer, especially in children. Then, other equally qualified scientists say the fears are exaggerated. So, who can you trust?

Despite denials by many scientists and large agribusinesses, there seems reason to be cautious.[16] Recently, a study that tested 957 non-organic foods found that 203 still had some pesticides, including nearly all of the bread tested. While the study claimed that the amounts found were safe, other scientists say our understanding of the effects of pesticides on human health is still very limited.

[16] **cautious:** careful to avoid harm

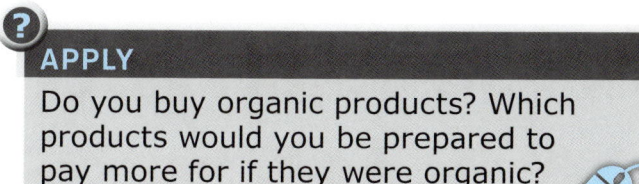

? APPLY

Do you buy organic products? Which products would you be prepared to pay more for if they were organic?

We don't really know the amount of pesticides we can safely consume. So it is probably a good idea to consume less of them. But can you afford to? Not everyone can pay the high prices necessary to buy organic food regularly. While organic eggs, for example, may cost only 50 percent more than the regular kind, an organic chicken can sometimes cost six times the price of a factory-farmed one.

It's easy to forget that without industrial farming methods, we simply wouldn't have so much cheap food. Are we prepared to give up meat every day and return to having it less frequently, like our grandparents did?

Of course, many people say we should. They provide not only health reasons but ethical and ecological ones, too. They argue that we have quickly gone from having too little food to having too much, and that we have become used to a way of life that is destroying our environment and harming our health. Their critics, on the other hand, say it's too **idealistic** to think we can produce the food the world needs organically.

The main problem with organics seems to be that although it opposes big business, it is also becoming big business. You may feel that the organic Indonesian oils in your shampoo do wonders for your hair. But shipping shampoo halfway across the world certainly isn't going to help stop the greenhouse effect. And does the supermarket selling it to you really care about the conditions of the workers who produce it? Many organic products are unsustainable. They may be good for us, but are they good for the planet? Perhaps we should be replacing the word "organic" with "local" and "hand-made." Or, perhaps, we should just do like some of our grandparents did and grow our own food.

Video Quest

New Organic Products

Watch this video about an organic drink. Why is this drink thought to be better than coffee?

CHAPTER 6

What Do You Think?

IS ORGANICS THE WAY FORWARD OR A DEAD END? WHICH ARGUMENTS DO YOU AGREE WITH THE MOST? AND THE LEAST?

A dead end!

Although many people claim that organic food tastes better, there is simply no evidence that the nutrients in the food are any different. A plant doesn't know whether the nitrogen it receives comes from manure or is artificial. Nitrogen is nitrogen is nitrogen. Organic food is simply an expensive way of selling the same products.

The way forward!

Organic foods are picked in season and grow slowly and naturally, unlike many industrially farmed foods, which are artificially forced. Rather than spending weeks or months in storage, they can be bought within days of being picked. This makes them fresher, tastier, and more **nutritious**.

A dead end!

Organic foods are just a status symbol that people buy in the same way they buy designer labels.

Nobody really needs organic produce.

The way forward!

Organic food can be a reality for everybody. People can get cheap food by supporting local producers, sharing with friends, and growing their own – even in the city! Cuba has shown us a lot can be done with very little.

A dead end!

There is no way we can feed the seven billion people on this planet using natural methods. Organic production would lead to starvation for half the planet. It is an idealistic luxury that only the wealthy can afford.

The way forward!

We cannot continue to produce food the way we do. The world's **resources** are limited. Traditional factory farming requires chemical fertilizers and machinery that both depend on oil. The coming oil crisis threatens this way of farming, and organic farming will be the only way forward once chemical resources are used up. It's better to start sooner rather than later.

After You Read

Read the questions and choose Ⓐ, Ⓑ, Ⓒ, or Ⓓ.

1 Why was Whole Foods Market successful?

Ⓐ It was cheaper than other stores.

Ⓑ It sold many different vegetables.

Ⓒ Because of the range of things it sold.

Ⓓ Because it was a big company.

2 What was considered to be one negative aspect of Whole Foods Market operations?

Ⓐ They didn't buy produce locally.

Ⓑ They didn't pay workers well.

Ⓒ They sold meat products.

Ⓓ They used harmful chemicals.

3 Who first used the word organic to refer to healthy food?

Ⓐ Justus von Liebig

Ⓑ Sir Albert Howard

Ⓒ Lord Northbourne

Ⓓ Norman Borlaug

4 What was Borlaug's main intention?

Ⓐ to become famous

Ⓑ to invent new technology

Ⓒ to win a Nobel prize

Ⓓ to produce more food

5 How did the owners of small farms try to gain a share of the market in the USA?

Ⓐ They sold their produce to the big supermarkets.

Ⓑ They tried to obtain the necessary certificates.

Ⓒ They joined together to sell to local people.

Ⓓ They told people the benefits of organic food.

6 How did Cuba overcome its food shortage problems after 1991?

(A) by exporting cigars and rum

(B) by going back to old farming methods

(C) by importing food from the U.S.A.

(D) by increasing production with chemicals

7 What is the main reason for the present day popularity of organic products?

(A) They are more fashionable.

(B) They are easily available.

(C) They do not contain chemicals.

(D) They do not cost as much.

Match

Match the information with the following four chapters.

A	B	C	D
Chapter 1	Chapter 3	Chapter 4	Chapter 5
Whole Foods	Agribusiness vs. Organic Farming	Organopónicos	Going Organic – Is It Worth It?

Which chapter refers to . . .

1 health risks of chemical pesticides? _____

2 organic products other than food? _____

3 escape from modern life? _____

4 government controlled urban gardens? _____

5 negative comments about a store? _____

6 a foreign trade embargo? _____

7 one small company becoming successful? _____

8 the fear of non-organic produce? _____

Answer Key

Words to Know, page 4
1 urban garden **2** whole foods **3** pest **4** fertilizer
5 soil

Words to Know, page 5
1 nutrients **2** critic **3** debate **4** activist **5** pioneer
6 ethical **7** pesticides

Predict, page 5
Answers will vary.

Evaluate, page 9
Answers will vary.

Video Quest, page 11
Possible answers: It's fresher. Your body receives the right
nutrients at the right time of year.

Video Quest, page 15
More than 28 hundred miles. Bringing food from far away
uses a lot of gas and produces carbon emissions.

Apply, page 21
Answers will vary.

Video Quest, page 23
It's stimulating, the same as coffee, but it's also rich in
nutrients, such as vitamins and minerals and antioxidants.

Choose the Correct Answers, page 26
1 C **2** A **3** C **4** D **5** C **6** B **7** C

Match, page 27
1 C **2** D **3** B **4** C **5** A **6** C **7** A **8** D